The Business of Social Media
Clients & Customers
Not Just Likes & Followers

Contents

Dedication

In my life, I love you more.

This book is possible because one man believed in me. He gave me the courage to jump when we had no idea what our future held, and he was ready and willing to go for the ride.

I love you Andy.

Thank you.

In the end, we only regret
the chances we didn't take.

Embracing the Power of Social Media

"Embrace change. Envision what could be,
challenge the status quo
and drive creative destruction." –Charles Koch

Three years ago, I was in a pure panic. My son had been born in May and I was less than three weeks away from having to go back to my full-time job as a retail store manager. There was this tiny little person who had been counting on me to do everything for him while my husband was at work and I had to make a decision that women make every day – do I quit my job to stay home and raise him or do I let someone else raise him for 40 hours a week? The idea of someone else taking on what I felt was my primary responsibility as a mom, had me in tears almost constantly. It was literally the night before I was to go back to work that my husband and I made the decision – I would stay home. No matter what financial difficulties lied ahead, we would weather the storm and I would find a way to make it work.

That was one of the hardest decisions I have ever had to make in my life. Not knowing the outcome, having faith that life will work out as intended, leaving a career that I had spent 18 years building and a solid future full of certainty to basically jump off a cliff into the ether blindfolded.

"You gain strength, courage and confidence by every experience in which you really stop to look fear in the face. You are able to say to yourself. I lived through this horror. I can take the next thing that comes along. "
– Eleanor Roosevelt

It was the best decision I have ever made. Has it been easy? Hell no. But worth it every day I look at my son and now my beautiful daughter because I did something to make sure I could stay home…I embraced the power of being social.

Social media was a world that I had avoided basically since its inception. I had a Facebook profile – because really, everyone I knew had one, but I wasn't active on it. It was more just there to show people I was alive and for me to look at my family's pictures. But when I made a decision to stay at home – I needed a new career and fast.

A few months earlier I had signed up to be a Beachbody coach. Now if you don't know what Beachbody is – think extreme workout programs, such as P90X, Insanity and the 21 Day Fix. I was already a very active runner and used these programs, so it made sense to focus my efforts on being a coach and helping others get in shape using these products.

Yet there was one HUGE problem. I didn't know a thing about how to act on social media and I had to figure it out rather quickly. We were going from a two-income family, down to one and I had always been the main breadwinner.

So I took the deep dive into social media. I spent hours each day taking online courses, listening to podcasts and watching YouTube videos on what to do on social media and just as importantly, what NOT to do on social media. How do you build an audience? How can you ensure you have the RIGHT audience? What do you do when people follow you and once you have a following – how do you turn that into a business?

#SocialExperience: You can't take back a Direct Message

I learned this the hard way. Once you send a message on Facebook messenger and I'm sure every other platform, it is there for them to see. There is no recalling of the message and if you delete it on your end, it's only gone on your end. So pay attention to what you write – read it multiple times for spelling errors, grammar issues and the like, because once it's out there, you can't take it back.

My deep dive into the world of social media for Beachbody provided me with a rather profound insight, if I had to do all this work to understand social media, how would an entrepreneur or small business person even have the time to spend a tenth of their day running their own social media presence? From that one thought bloomed the career I now have, one that at that time was just an idea and now has become a college major. Crazy how life works out eh?

This book is about showing you what I learned at the beginning and the experiences I have gained over the past few years by helping entrepreneurs and businesses to improve and/or create their own social media profiles. I will teach you the skills you need to not only create a consistent digital presence but how to ensure that whether you have 100 followers or 100,000, that you are creating a cash flow into your business. Because lets face it – what good are thousands, even millions of followers if they aren't actually paying clients?

Social media is about pitching to your niche, knowing your target market and focusing in on that group of people. Can you have multiple target markets? Yes and no, an undefined group can muddy the waters. If you cast your net too wide then you may not get the results you are seeking, yet if it's too narrow you may not reach your full potential.

I worked in retail for over 18 years and as a (mostly) silent partner in my husband's home brew supply shop, I am still speaking with customers daily. This contact with your customers, in person or online, is invaluable. I have been targeting customers for marketing purposes and sales for almost my entire working life.

I started as an intern for a small film company in Santa Monica, CA working the Internet and at the time the world of MySpace, to promote a film that had been released to video. This was partnered with us traveling the entire west coast and visiting EVERY Hollywood Video from San Diego to Seattle where we randomly approached people and talked about the movie. If I had ever had any reservations about becoming a sales person, I got over it that summer.

That summer taught me that you not only needed to present your product for those to see, but to make sure that you went out and found people that would be interested as well. That finding people part? That's what 90% of small businesses fail to do on social media. It is so ingrained that people come to us, that this shift in marketing that has happened over the past five years is throwing many companies for a loop.

#SocialKEY – Marketing today is different. It's building relationships and attracting YOUR clients.

You need to attract, interact and FIND your ideal prospective clients and customers. Marketing has changed and its demanding time as well as money.

At one time I worked for small retail businesses where I was a clothing buyer, chief marketing officer, sales person and manager. In this environment, your relationship with your customer defined what you did on an everyday basis. What promotions you might be running and how you set up the store. If you moved a product to the front of the store because it wasn't selling, or just folded it differently to showcase it on a different wall or shelf for exposure.

These same techniques were used when I was at H&M, Tommy Hilfiger and Eddie Bauer. I have doubled the volume of stores in less than two years by simply increasing product and knowing what my customers wanted. Navigating the landscape of social media is no different.

Do you KNOW what your customers want? REALLY know what makes them tick?

Every day, and I mean EVERYDAY, I am re-evaluating my customers plans. How often am I posting? Does it need to be more often or less? What type of content am I curating for them? Do we have enough organic content? Am I using the new tools that the platforms have given me?

#SocialFAIL – Never stopping to refine your strategy.

The definition of insanity is to do the same thing over and over again and expect different results. Social media has its own version of crazy and I have had my share of failures as I have navigated this intense world. One of my first was to post, post, post and post some more, without any thought as to what my clients wanted to see. It's not about you or your business anymore, it's about your customers.

These are the thoughts that run through my head on a daily basis - this is also why people hire me to run their social media.

Most businesses are focused on refining their products, teaching their sales force the new ins and outs of a technique and working on managing the day to day running of a business. I know that this is not easy! My past in running retail stores and now running three online businesses reminds me daily that if I don't focus, and I don't delegate, that I am not helping my clients, I am losing them.

Can you do social media on your own? Absolutely. The question I always ask my prospects is simple – ***just because you can do something, should you?***

Should you waste your valuable time doing something that you are okay at, when you could focus on what you are excellent at? You could build your business doing what you love while someone else takes on the stuff you just like.

Delegation is the key to success and sanity for entrepreneurs and businesses. As passionate people (all entrepreneurs are either passionate or crazy, or a bit of both) we love to dive in to every aspect of our business, yet we need to focus on what we do well, and allow others to do what they do, to help us truly grow.

Those customers that you are seeking daily? They are out there. They are ready to buy whatever product or service you are looking to sell them. You need to focus, know your niche, your vital priorities and find them. How will you do that? By getting into what I call, the LONG GAME.

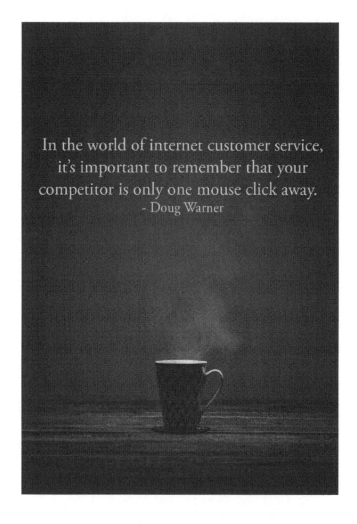

In the world of internet customer service,
it's important to remember that your
competitor is only one mouse click away.
- Doug Warner

Seeking More Business? Know Your Client

"Everyone is NOT your customer." – Seth Godin

Before we talk about the Long Game and the timeline for getting a social media presence moving for your business, we need to talk about one of the major mistakes that people, myself included, make on social media time and time again.

The biggest mistake that people make on social media is posting for their business and failing to post for their target demographic.

Your target demographic is the group of people that want to buy your product, service, etc.

People that actually want to see and are searching for the services that you are providing.

Social media marketing is awareness marketing. I'm going to be a broken record on this one - It's not like marketing of the past. No longer do we put out a magazine ad praying for a two to three percent return on investment, hoping that the right people will see our ad. Praying that this time we advertised in the right magazine, or put up the right billboard to catch our customer's eye, no, today you can target exactly the type of person you want - as long as you know who that is.

Knowing your target market or demographic is something that most companies never completely define. For some reason or another it is not something that they focus on. They want to share what is amazing about their company. We save the planet, we have the best shoes in the world, I can show you how to sell a house tomorrow with little to no investment...do these things sound familiar?

More than likely.

Everyone loves to talk about themselves. It's a human nature weakness, yet the question is, does your customer care about what you are putting out there? Do they care if they are the best shoes in the world if they don't wear shoes? Really, my sister lives steps from the ocean and rarely wears anything on her feet other than sandals, and that's not that frequently. So if you are advertising to a beach community, are you really going to get an influx of business? Probably not.

#SocialFAIL – Talk about how amazing your business is repeatedly in your posts, creating a brag board.

I hate to break it to you, but no one really cares about you or your business. They care about what you can do for THEM. How can what you do benefit your client or customer you are seeking? Don't create a brag board and only post about your product or service. Post about things that will interest your clients and make sense with your brand.

These are questions that we don't ask ourselves enough about our businesses. Not just what do I want people to know about me and my company, but what do I know about the customers I want? A very smart woman by the name of Chalene Johnson had a theory that I have expanded upon and created a clear step by step process to determine your exact target market – what I call, your Power 5. Because, contrary to what we all believe, everyone is not your customer.

First Step – Think about your five best customers.

If every customer you had were just like these people then you would have the most successful business, with people that you love to work with and the world would be full of cupcakes and rainbows.

Second Step – What characteristics do these people have in common?

This is a bit trickier. This is where you get into the details. Are they entrepreneurs? Stay at home moms? Work from home freelancers? Working professionals? Tradesmen or women? Parents? Dog lovers? Pet lovers of any kind? Relationship status?

19

College Educated? Income level? What cars do they drive? Where do they go on vacations? Where do they stay when they go? What type of homes do they have? Do they have more than one home?

Think about every aspect of their lives that you know to help you get a complete picture.

Third Step – Build your Ideal customer.

Take all of the information that you have about your 5 best customers that you came up with in step two and create your Ideal Customer.

Name them and create a life for them. For example – Suzy Sales is a mom of two middle school aged children who go to a private school, married, she works from home as the owner of a small advertising company.

She has a Bachelor's degree in Communications from a small community college and loves soccer and running. They have one dog at home, a purebred shepherd, and travel frequently. Her husband loves craft beer and they often take trips to Napa Valley, CA for the wine tastings. They drive a Subaru and when they aren't traveling for beer or wine, they are camping to explore nature and in the winter travel to the best downhill ski hills both domestically and abroad.

They have disposable income and enjoy spending it on the things and experiences that matter to them - such as vacations, wine, craft beer, races for running, improving their home and landscaping and sports for their kids.

Fourth Step – What are the 5 things that you want customers to know about your company?

Are you honest and trustworthy? Provide exceptional customer service? Are you flexible in your product or service offerings? What products or services do you offer? What are the foundations of your company – charity, causes, etc that you stand for?

These 5 things should be unique to your business. For example, every bar has beer and televisions, so don't focus on what makes you the same as every other bar - what does your business have or do that no one else does?

Fifth Step – Now is where the magic starts – you put them all together to create your posting strategy.

Think about your ideal customer - what they would like to see and what you want people to know. Then you can marry what you want people to know about your company into posts. Those are the things you post about. ONLY those.

Don't try to overdo your page. Stick to what will appeal to your customers. Your categories should be broad enough that it will cover a range of articles and images, while showing your brand personality.

Below is an example of VENTUREWRITE's
posting strategy and how to put it all together.

Power of 5

5 Best Customers

1) Lincoln D
2) Sally Sales
3) Julie Fox
4) Michael Xavier
5) Angela Denton

5 Customer Characteristics

1) Entrepreners
2) Parents
3) Honest
4) Always on the go
5) Social Media Savvy

Top 5 About You

1) Social Maven
2) Content Writer
3) Results Driven
4) Constantly Learning
5) Graphic Excellence

Posting Strategy

1) Newest Social Updates
2) Kids & Social/Safety
3) How to Measure Results with Social
4) Writing Best Practices for Biz Marketing
5) Motivational & Productivity Tips for Entrepreneurs

Your posting strategy, knowing what to post about, and what NOT to post about is key to a clear brand image and concise page. You need to know who you are working to attract before any step can be made on social media.

> ## #SocialKEY – Know WHO you are trying to attract BEFORE you post!
>
> If you aren't targeted in on your core client demographic, then your page will fail. I've seen it happen multiple times. Focus on your clients and customers and they will reward you for it.

We spend so much time thinking about WHAT to post that we fail to really dial in on WHO we want to buy our products or could find our services useful. That is the real trick of social – **you want**

to attract clients and customers more than just add another like or follower to your account.

The world of marketing has changed, and you can adapt to conquer it.

Now, you may be asking, why did I create the client Suzy Sales? All that information - dogs, running, outdoors, craft beer, etc. Those are aspects of personalities that you can use in your images for your company.

Remember, you want people to share images from your page. Creating an image with a computer isn't necessarily exciting, but a woman sitting on the edge of a vineyard with a wine glass thinking about how to improve her business? That has the possibility to go viral. An image of a family walking their dog with some quote about how social media can work while you spend time with your family? Perfect to share.

Every time you create anything for social media you should be thinking – would SUZY share this? Because remember, it's not you that we are worried about. It's Suzy and what is attracting HER. Suzy is the one scrolling her newsfeed thinking about how to improve her business, or maybe just mindlessly scrolling through her feed at the end of a crazy day with the kids – what will make Suzy stop her feed and take action? Because action (a like, comment or share) is how your business begins to build online.

The Long Game - Social Media Success Does NOT Happen Overnight

"Strive not to be a success but rather to be of VALUE." – Albert Einstein

Social Media Marketing is not something that happens overnight. Those "overnight sensations" – didn't really happen overnight. It took years of hard work to get noticed. Does it have to take years? No.

But my point is this - don't expect social media to work immediately.

You might get a new follower or like on your page, but you may not have anyone actually come to your business right away. People imagine that the right social media platform can bring them millions, and it might, but it needs TIME.

Social media is a courtship.

Social Media is a tool that is used to build relationships between potential customers and yourself and it can take a minimum of SIX MONTHS to see any type of major traction. That is to merely find a baseline. Six months of consistent posting, creating content and talking to others on your chosen social media platforms.

But you can't post and just forget it. There is so much more to social media than knowing what to post. After you have your posting strategy in hand, you populate your page with excellent content, but where does the magic happen? When you go out and seek prospective clients. How do you do this? ***Engagement.***

To engage successfully on social media, you need to be present and focused on your customer. Go out and like other pages and join groups – things that Suzy would be interested in. She likes German shepherds, go find a dog page or group or focus on the entrepreneur aspect - is there a networking group you can join or maybe you are a runner as well, join a running group and like the local run shop's page.

Once you have identified places on your platform that Suzy and those like Suzy may be hanging out, you can begin to engage. This is where everyone seems to panic – I don't know what to say!

Say hello.

It's really that simple. Okay, don't just say hello. Depending on the page that might be creepy. But take this example - if a page has a post about a puppy then tell them how adorable it is. **DO NOT, and I repeat DO NOT put some sort of contact me for XYZ service in the**

comments. That will get you banned from the page and marked forever as a spammer.

Commenting on posts and liking them is how you will build a relationship. Maybe the person posting the puppy picture isn't exactly interested in what you do, but they might respond, and you can start a conversation. Or someone might see your comment or like and head over to your page to see what you are doing. They might like your page. They might find you on other social platforms to see what is going on with your business. Social media is like the Kevin Bacon game – every actor can be somehow tied back to Kevin Bacon in six steps. I'm dating myself, but really, try it.

The point is that you need to interact with people and pages. You need to build a community around your page and brand. Find out what is going on with your customers – ask them questions. What do they want to see more of?

What would they like to see a blog about? Post a survey – chose A, B or C and give options. Create a contest to entice them to interact with you or post to your page, or even share your page.

One of my favorite things to do to increase engagement with a post is to tell people to tag a friend who is an entrepreneur or maybe tag someone who would benefit from this post. That brings more people to your page and your favorite customers are helping to spread the word – you are creating raving fans.

Why do you want raving fans? Because they make your life much, much easier.

They spread the word for you. They will tell people about how they love your product and/or service and why. They will share their experiences online and in person with passion. Having someone with this amount of loyalty to your brand is INVALUABLE. It is a known fact that someone will take the advice of a friend over that of the expert or professional, 9 out of 10 times, so you need these types of fans.

One of the best examples of this type of loyalty from fans is an Apple consumer. I am personally an Apple fan, so I understand this loyalty, almost devout reverence for all things Apple...and I am not alone. I have an iPhone, an iPad, an iPad mini and a MacBook Pro. I honestly, don't' know how to work most things PC and when I find someone using one, I will ask them why? Why are they not living in the wonderful world of Apple products? I must help them see why Apple is such a fantastic company and the products are an excellent investment.

The people who use Apple products truly do not understand why you would ever switch to something that is not an Apple product. They believe that they have the best things available, or will when the next upgrade comes out, and switching is almost sacrosanct. Steve Jobs did not set out to create this type of consumer base, but he did, and it is something to be studied and if at all possible, replicated.

Attracting these types of loyal fans cannot be measured; its value is truly priceless.

This type of fan however, does not necessarily happen overnight. You need to romance them. Share excellent content, create beautiful images to be shared and most importantly, deliver superior customer service online and in person.

If this sounds like it's a lot of work, then you are correct, it is. That's why I have a business that does nothing but manage social media.

I have a client who is a plumber. He is phenomenal in what he does and is at his shop day and night. He has to deal with the fact that tradesmen are at an all-time low (we will be screwed one day when no one wants to be a plumber) and his phones are blowing up 24/7.

This didn't happen overnight. He started to get calls from women who said he had heard about his business through one of their mommy groups.

Mommy groups? Yes. He had no idea what they were talking about, but knew he had to capitalize on this and reached out to me. He had no desire to learn about Facebook, his business was doing well, but now, after being on social media for two years, his business is booming.

I will ask him to run an ad every month and almost every time he will tell me no because he is afraid his business will explode even further because he can barely keep up with the current demand. That is music to my ears.

It isn't about likes with his Facebook page or followers on his Twitter account, it's about how many people are clicking the call now button. It's about answering questions and attracting the right market. It's about finding the moms and instilling trust in his business. He doesn't have time to do that, he doesn't need to, he has my team and me.

#SocialFAIL: Give away content for free

Often digital experts will tell you that you need to give to get. To some extent I believe that. A blog is free. Whitepapers are full of valuable information and are seen as free – but are they? Not really, you need to give your email to get that information and that is invaluable for an online marketer. If you don't get monetary value from a prospective client, get their email or some way to contact them. Because whatever you are providing has a value, don't just give it all away for free and wait til later to monetize it.

There's no shortage of remarkable ideas, what's missing is the will to execute them.
- Seth Godin

Maximize Your ROI on Social Media – A Step by Step Guide

"Get closer than ever to your customers. So close that you tell them what they need well before they realize it themselves." – Steve Jobs

Posting on your platforms and engaging with customers are the two biggest pieces of running any type of online digital presence, but that is not all. Here are samples of daily and weekly checklists that I have created for my clients when I coach them on how to create a solid digital presence on just a few of the major platforms.

DAILY Checklist to Embrace Social Power

Facebook

- ☐ Ensure Posts from scheduler have posted
- ☐ Engage other users on platform – comment, like and/or share posts on 5 to 10 accounts a day
- ☐ LIKE one page with high engagement
- ☐ Share one post per day from top engagement pages
- ☐ Respond to all messages

Twitter

- ☐ Identify new followers from Notifications
  - ○ Send Thank You for following tweet to all new followers
    - ▪ Can batch thank you, but never more than 3 or 4 in a tweet

☐ Send Direct Messages to ALL new followers if not automated

  o Include link to Freemium (E-book, whitepaper, etc) on pop up page for email address – "Thank you for following! Here is a free gift for you (insert link)"

☐ Respond to ALL Direct Messages

  o People will thank you for following – send them the link to your freemium and site if you have not done so already

☐ Comment/Like/Re-tweet based on searches for hashtags or specific people

☐ Follow people daily

  o Use the account of influencers to identify their followers and follow others who are influential in their list

- o Remember the rule of thirds – for every 300 you follow, 100 will follow you back – work to follow 100 new people daily
- ☐ Add new followers to your Lists

Instagram:

- ☐ Follow 5 – 10 new accounts per day
  - o Double tap on 4-5 images and Comment on One to encourage engagement and follow-back
  - o Ask a question if you can
- ☐ Ensure use of hashtags that can be searched
- ☐ Research and Use hashtags of key demographic on posts
- ☐ Post Once a Day - minimum

Pinterest

- ☐ Pin new links and/or images
  - o The exact amount does not matter. It is the presence daily and adding to your boards that is important with this platform
- ☐ Like and/or comment on 5 to 10 pinners
- ☐ Follow 5 to 10 new accounts

WEEKLY To Do List for Social Success

☐ Record and Analyze Metrics from all Social Media Platforms

☐ Identify Top Post/Tweet/Pin

☐ Refine Strategy for the following week to include similar posts/tweets/pins to the Top Post/Tweet/Pin

☐ Review Timelines on Facebook and Twitter
  o Do you have a variety of posts/tweets?
    ▪ IE: Images/Links/Posts from other influencers/Quotes

☐ Review timing and amount of posts on all platforms. Should we adjust our posting times – move them later in the day, earlier, etc. and should we be posting more or less for top engagement and reach

☐ Identify Top Influencer on Each Platform and ensure sharing from their account

☐ Schedule 90% of Facebook Posts
- o Ensure variety – balance images/links/quotes, posts with images and those without, etc
- o Other 10% should be live sharing from other pages or in the moment posts of current events

☐ Schedule Weekly Tweets for Twitter
- o Include Re-tweets and Quoted Tweets in Schedule
- o Ensure variety - balance images/links/quotes, posts with images and those without, etc
- o Ensure you have organic posts as well – more is better

- ☐ Un-follow and identify spam accounts or inactive accounts using Manageflitter or a similar tool
  - ○ Give people 7 days to follow-back and never un-follow on a Sunday

- ☐ Check source links on top Pins on Pinterest to ensure click through is correct and not broken

- ☐ Analyze Google Analytics on Social accounts to identify top platform
  - ○ What are you doing that is working on this platform?
  - ○ How can you replicate this type of success on the others?
  - ○ Do you need to expand into a similar platform?
    - ▪ IE: Facebook is doing well – expand to Twitter or Pinterest is doing well – expand to Instagram

- o Which platform is bringing in the most revenue?
- o Should we invest more in advertising here?
- o Should we up the amount of posts per day/week?
- ☐ What platform is performing below expectations?
  - o Identify worst performing posts/tweets/pins – eliminate them from future postings
  - o How can you improve this platform?
    - ▪ Quality of posts/tweets/pins?
  - o Quantity of posts/tweets/pins?
  - o Get influencers involved?
  - o Create a partnership with other bloggers/influencers to share their information and have them share yours

Once a MONTH – update cover photo on all applicable platforms

#SocialKEY: A minimum of 6 hours a week of time invested into social media is needed for true growth of any brand.

Yes, you can do the minimum amount of time and create an "existence" platform, but without interacting and creating unique, valuable content for your target audience, you will not see valuable results from your social media efforts.

The amount of work that needs to be put into an online social presence for any type of company can be mind-boggling. The list above doesn't even include the extremely necessary part of creating solid content and finding other content to share!

It is just the basic steps needed to maintain and grow an online digital presence. The above lists can easily take up to 4 hours per platform per week. I advise all my clients that you need a minimum of 6 hours per week on social media. Less than that is an existence platform.

Sure, you can only work 2 hours a week per platform, but that is baseline creation of maybe a few images and curated articles. No interaction and no type of organic, expert created content.

Two hours will do nothing to grow your business. It will give you a presence, but you will not thrive. The question that needs to be answered is simple – do you want your company to exist or thrive?

If you are reading this book, then my guess is that you want your business to thrive and kick ass on your way to the top.

Welcome, because so do I.

Return on Investment (ROI) is a number that we talk about in social media in regard to how much business you get back from your monetary investment in social media – and it should be quantified. The ever-present question is - how?

The first measurement and testing of ROI can immediately be seen when your reach and awareness level among your target client market is doubled, if not tripled. In many of my clients first few months on social media we quadrupled the amount of people who had been exposed to their brand.

"The ROI of social media is that your business will still exist in 5 years." –Erik Qualman, Author of Socialnomics

Below are examples of how different clients of mine measure their ROI. Each one is based on their unique business goals and their clients.

GOAL: Build Awareness so when the season changes, the phone is ringing.

One of my clients is a heating and air conditioning company. They had a dead page when we took over with an average of 10 – 17 unique individuals viewing content posted by them. We increased this number to 149 on the very first day we took over and have created a consistent audience of over 350 daily unique views since then. That is 350 unique people that have at some point seen this client's name that would not have seen it if they were not using their online presence. We ran an ad to increase this number and for less than $40, over 27,000 people were introduced to my client. 27,000 targeted individuals who owned a home or business and are likely to need my client's services at some time in the future.

That example was merely one of awareness and I have the same story for every client we have ever worked with – your brand name immediately becomes more recognizable when you begin to work your digital presence.

What about the real hard numbers? Actual clients knocking on the door?

Depending on your objective it can take a varying degree of effort and focus to deliver solid ROI. Here are a few examples of different objectives from my clients.

GOAL: Increase enrollment

A Montessori school was stretching for full enrollment for the new school year when we began working with them. We work 100% organically and have yet to run one Facebook ad. After one year of working the account we had two wonderful results – their annual fundraiser was attended by more people and earned an additional $4,000 and we did not have to advertise for classes for the following year. EVERY spot was filled without any additional advertising and a wait list had to be created for their summer camp and the next fall.

GOAL: Increase Advisor Appointments

A financial firm was looking to drive people in the door. Through a digital strategy including Facebook, Instagram and Twitter and a combination of ads, we have consistently had five to ten new appointments made with advisors every week! These are qualified solid leads that have turned into excellent business for this client.

The financial firm's results were after a year of consistent and solid content with a focused and directed ad campaign on both Facebook and Twitter. Most of this ad budget however, isn't usually spent on an ad for making appointments – it is used to promote their unique content and expertise in their field. They are used to spread awareness and increase the likelihood that an individual in their ideal market will click the link to make an appointment.

GOAL: Increase class participants

A home brew supply shop began running small ads - $20 for a boost of an upcoming BrewU class. Immediately they began filling every spot in their classes. For less than the cost of one participant, they were attracting the exact potential clients and filling their classes – almost every time. Ten class participants for the price of one - you can easily see the ROI here.

Until recently they have only used Facebook as a solid resource for filling their Brew U classes. Due to the impressive results of the ads for classes, they are increasing their presence on Facebook, Instagram and Twitter to drive more foot traffic to their store.

GOAL: Increasing awareness and client applications

Fitness consultants dabbled with their Facebook page and have had a hard time keeping a consistent presence. Initially they were focused on cold calling and were running out of prospects. We decided to change their strategy – increase their presence on their Facebook page and connect it to their Instagram account for ads. Run a small budget of less than $100 a month for consistent targeted reach and interact with other pages.

In less than 60 days of implementing the new strategy they had over 100, targeted moms seeking fitness, click on their application for their fitness crews and secured 3 new clients. This strategy has given them the one thing that they wanted more than anything else – TIME. They are two working moms who do this on the side and they needed the time with their families and warm leads. With our strategy we were able to deliver exactly what they needed, increasing their reach and client list.

These are only a few of the real results that my clients have seen from an active, consistent digital strategy. We have invested the time to determine the exact needs of every client and focused on what their company's goals are, focusing our actions to ensure results.

Each client has their own individual goals and what they determine is a solid ROI. They have reaped the benefits in sales – actual clients and customers walking in the door. Plus an intangible benefit - an influx of TIME.

One question that I repeatedly ask clients – how much is your time worth?

How much is your team's time worth?

If you were to take one or two people away from their current functions to run your social media presence – how much lost productivity would you have? Is that really the best use of their time? Do they know exactly how to put into action the needed digital strategy your company requires to get results?

Running a successful social media presence is a skill that just like any skill; can be taught. Can you do it yourself? Sure. But what else won't be getting done while you are worrying about what to post on Facebook?

Will you miss a call with a client? Will a prospective client fail to go on your prospecting list because you aren't focused on the actions that drive your bottom line? These are questions that face every business.

#SocialFAIL – Not knowing your business goals

When I first started working other accounts it became devastatingly clear that a business needed to know what they wanted from their social media. Yes, everyone wanted business, but that looks very different to each company. I have had my share of pages fail because the strategy was based on getting as many likes as possible, versus post what we need to get foot traffic in the door or push the call to action button.

Your business goals will determine how you use social media. If you do not know your goals, then social media will be like throwing spaghetti at the wall.

So my question to you is this – what are your business goals?

Now, the common answer I receive when I ask this question is "more business". Everyone wants that. So, my challenge to you right now is to think a little differently.

What type of business do you own and what do you really want? Is it more traffic to your website? Once there, how many people do you think you could convert? Do you want more sales at your Amazon store? Once people find your product on Amazon do they buy immediately, or do they get sucked into the other suggested products? What about feedback from your prospective clients? Are you launching a new product soon? Would more people attending your events be beneficial?

These questions are critical to your measurements of success. Without knowing exactly where you would like to go, no amount of social media advertising is going to help you. Why? Glad you asked.

Social Media is only one aspect of your overall marketing strategy and a tool, that, just like your target market, can be adjusted to fit your business needs.

Social Media is first and foremost an awareness tool and traffic driver. If you are seeking to send more people to your website or increase the overall awareness of your business, then social media should be your number one marketing tool.

Determining the ROI for traffic is fairly simple if you have the right tools in place. If you are sending your prospective clients to your website then you need Google analytics. You can add this to your website yourself and it will give you baseline numbers. A web designer can actually go in and optimize your site for analytics by making sure certain things are turned off on your site, meaning that clicks won't be measured from certain IP addresses (you don't want to measure your own team going to your site) and ensure that other IP addresses are being measured. To really know more about this – go ask a web designer. I have a few excellent people I can recommend, yet personally, I focus on what I am good at, and that is not website programming.

Once your site is set up with Google Analytics you will be able to see where your website traffic is coming from. There is a specific tab on the bottom called Social – this is where it will tell you exactly where your customers clicked on the link to arrive at your site - Facebook, Twitter, LinkedIn, Instagram, Pinterest, etc. It could be only one visit from a social media site and it will show you where they went on your site and how long they stayed there.

If your goal is to send them to your Amazon store then it is a bit trickier to measure. Why? Because once they go into the Amazon ether you lose all of your tracking ability. But have no fear - there are other ways to measure.

Knowing where you want your clients to go – your end game – is paramount in ROI determination. If you are sending them somewhere without the ability to track, then you need to take stock of the actions that your prospects are making within the social platforms, this is where the analytics from each platform come into play.

Every platform gives you three baseline measurement tools. How many new followers or likes your account received that week, the engagement level on your posts and your overall reach or impressions on the platform.

Engagement level is the amount of comments, likes, shares or any other actions that a post receives. I have a baseline engagement average goal of 5 to 10 engagements for 50% of posts on an active and well performing page.

Reach/Impressions is how many people saw your posts in their newsfeed or possibly went directly to your profile. To gain a solid ROI you need to first develop a tool to measure your stats. Below are the main items to measure from Facebook, Twitter, Pinterest, Instagram and LinkedIn.

- *Facebook*
  - LIKES gained this week
  - Weekly Post Reach
  - Weekly Post Engagement
  - The Week's Number One Post & its organic reach
  - Ads Created this Week
    - Ad Reach – Paid

- Ad Reach – Organic
- Results from Ad
  - Traffic from FB to website via Google Analytics
  - Sales converted from FB customers
  - Goals for each metric

- *Twitter*
  - Followers Added
  - Number of accounts Following
  - Top Follower and their reach
  - Tweet Impressions
  - Mentions
  - Top Engagement Tweet
  - Traffics from Twitter to website via Google Analytics
  - Sales converted from Twitter customers
  - Goals for each metric

- Instagram
  - Followers Added

- ▪ Total People Followed that Week
- ▪ Top Engager
- ▪ Top Hashtag that had excellent Engagement

- o *Pinterest*
  - ▪ Followers gained
  - ▪ Top Saved Pin
  - ▪ Top Engaged Pin
  - ▪ Top click through Pin
  - ▪ Avg Daily Impressions
  - ▪ Avg Daily Viewers
  - ▪ Avg Monthly Viewers
  - ▪ Avg Monthly Engaged
  - ▪ Traffic driven to website
  - ▪ Sales converted from Pinterest customers
  - ▪ Goals for each metric

- o LinkedIn
  - ▪ How many people have viewed your profile

- Views of Post (reach)
- Most popular post
- New contacts gained
- Sales converted from contacts

Once you have created your tracker you have the baseline numbers to determine your success based upon your goals. If it is more business that you are seeking from your social media platforms then there is one extra step that you need to take – you need to track where your leads came from in house.

Google Analytics will tell you how many people have visited your site and you can even follow through to see if they have purchased via your website. However, if you are a service based business or do not have the option to sell your products via your website, then you need to get that information from your clients when they call or stop in to your business. Simply asking: "How did you hear about us?" to a new customer will tell you where your greatest investment in marketing efforts should go.

Now that you have the baselines down – let's look at where the real magic happens.

Ads. Facebook ads to be specific.

To be clear, almost every platform has the option for ads. In my experience, currently, the targeting of Facebook far surpasses any of the other platforms. One bonus – since Facebook owns Instagram, you can often run ads on both platforms for the same price.

A client in the finance industry has a tricky game to play on social. They can't benefit from reviews or check in's because the US Federal government doesn't allow members of the finance industry to receive them. Really. We had to remove that option from every social media platform they are on. The finance industry cannot provide advice on-line in a traditional sense. Working closely with this client, we created a strategy using Facebook, Twitter and Instagram that is currently producing over 45 unique visitors to their website monthly.

That isn't just traffic from their social platforms, but people that are contacting their office to set up appointments. This is all from an original strategy that up until now was only producing one to two leads a month. What changed? We layered in ads.

If you have heard that a Facebook ad doesn't work, then you aren't using it correctly. Sorry. I will have some ads that go crazy and others that fall flat within 48 hours. If they aren't giving me solid results, I pull them and try again. So where do you start?

With the end in mind.

#SocialKEY: Facebook ads work

You need to know how to run them, when to run them and who to target every time you set up to run one. This can be either one of the easiest things to do on social media or one of the hardest. Which is why many clients hire me and my team – to make it easy on themselves and provide consistent results.

There is a strategy to social media ads that work. You need to be focused and ensure that your ad calendar not only aligns with your business goals, but it aligns with your business and community events. Again, begin with the end in mind.

What do you want to do? This is how Facebook has set up their ad platform. Do you want more traffic to your site, or more likes on your Facebook page? Do you want greater engagement from the fans already on your page or do you want people to go to your Amazon site or another website off of Facebook? These goals determine how you will set up your ads.

Once you have determined where you want to drive your prospective clients then you need to set your target audience. This is where you really need to get specific. You may think that the wider the net you cast the more return you will get on your investment, not on social. People are like squirrels. I'm not kidding. How long is our attention span? About a nanosecond. No one has time to pay attention to something that in some way, shape or form is not going to benefit them.

Your ad needs to be specific and easy for your target niche to take action.

I recently had a client tell me that they have so many different demographics because they have a variety of products. That's great! Make an ad for each one. But don't try to hit everyone with the same ad. The image and copy should be different for each target audience. It should be so compelling that it will immediately gain someone's attention and they will take action.

Facebook allows you to set up an audience with everything from individual's interest levels to their income and net worth.

I have one client who does security for homes in a very wealthy area of the North Shore (Chicago's Northern Suburbs where many professional athletes and prominent business people live). When they initially began running ads they couldn't figure out why they were getting people completely outside of their target market to like their page. They wanted investment bankers and they were getting those in inner city Chicago making $25,000 or less a year. The problem? They hadn't defined their market correctly. Once we added in income levels and net worth amounts they started to get solid traction and the type of attention that they wanted.

We also ran a specific ad for this client based on Spring Break. We knew people were going to be going on vacation and they were looking to hone in on new clients for their house watching service. We were able to send over 300 leads to their website within a two-week period because not only did we determine the correct audience, but we were also able to hone in on those going on vacation.

How did we know? Because Facebook targeted those that had recently checked out a travel app, those that had recently made reservations for flights or those that were frequent travelers. Our ad was so dialed in that we were able to attract exactly whom we wanted and send them to their site.

This was fantastic! Yet a note of caution and why I will tell you that social media is only one part of your marketing strategy. We sent over 300 leads to their website – can you guess how many calls they received? None. Not one call.

This of course led us to dig deeper, because we knew that it wasn't our Facebook efforts that had failed – it was where they had ended up.

The website page was not welcoming and to some seemed very intimidating. Our kink in the marketing funnel was the website and something that needed to be addressed. Sometimes you don't know these things until you have great success in other areas of your marketing. For us, it was a lesson learned.

#SocialFAIL: Using Ads as Click Bait

One of the worst things you can do with a Facebook ad is to send someone to the wrong page. Do not and I repeat, DO NOT have a picture and a tag line about signing up for some specific XYZ whitepaper and then send them to the home page of your website or some other page. Each ad should have a landing page or specific page associated with it to ensure that your intended market is getting exactly where they need to be with ONE CLICK. This builds trust and credibility with your business, and honestly, it is annoying to the end user and unprofessional for the page to send people to the wrong spot when you have worked so hard to get them to click the link in the first place.

Besides the click through rate on your ad, or Likes on your page, Facebook will give your ad a relevance score. This score will tell you how important your ad is to the market you have defined. It is from 1 – 10, with 1 being not relevant and 10 being very relevant. I try to stick to having an ad with a score of 7 or above. If it doesn't get there within 48 to 72 hours then I will scrap it and set up a new ad.

One other tool that is very important for you to use is the Facebook pixel. This little piece of code can be put on any website page to track an ad and receive exact insights on whether the ad is working. You can do it yourself - they have tutorials on it or have your web designer add it to the correct page.

Each ad can have a unique set up using your account pixel, so just know that this is a step that will need to be verified and double checked with every ad sending people to your website.

Another important note when sending people to websites off of Facebook – make sure you send them to the correct page.

Nothing is more annoying than clicking on a link that says it will take you to more information on a free recipe book and instead you are directed to the main page of the website, searching for where you want to go. More than likely you will lose that prospect and they will have a bad taste in their mouth because in their mind, you have tricked them. No one likes click bait – and that is the definition of it.

It is extremely important to constantly monitor and measure your ads. You do not want to spend money without seeing a consistent return. And yes, I have noticed that the more money you spend on Facebook, the greater your return. If you have an ad for a highly sought after audience and you only spend $5 on the ad, then you may have very little return. How do you know if $5 is too little? Test and measure - because to be honest, you don't. You can have a really good idea depending on how many people you can reach – Facebook gives you a handy little demographic meter, but unless you actually invest the time and money into the ad campaign you have no idea what your return may be. Yet for me, that's the fun part.

I love the strategy and the ever-changing world of social media. It's what excites me about a new post or a new client. My goal is to always increase the clients business in some way, shape or form. I want to drive traffic and increase awareness while they can continue to do what they do – work their business and close the leads my team is sending their way. I thrive in organized chaos and that is the world of social media. It's why many of my clients look to me and my team for social success. Because discovering the correct social strategy, the willingness to try until we succeed, and changing it all again when it gets stale - that is where my passion truly resides.

My passion also excels in the world of failure. Or as some people will say – the test and measure aspect.

To be fair, it took me a long time to be comfortable with failing. If you listen to all the big wig personal development gurus, failing forward is a big catch phrase. I'm not sure why, but failing seemed horrifying no matter what spin you put on it.

Then one day, I got it.

It wasn't the failing aspect (really, for me that part still sucks) but it was the after aspect. The hindsight is 20/20, where I could reflect and say what didn't work. That was the part I have been doing my whole life. It didn't work this way, so what about if we do it just a little differently, will we get a different result? This is the definition of failing forward.

If it didn't work the first time, try, try again until you succeed. That's a much nicer way than saying failing forward, don't you think?

But what does this have to do with ads? It is the entire basis of Facebook ads or any type of social media marketing. They may or may not work all the time, but you need to try, because they will provide amazing results - when done correctly.

Now, the next question that always comes up is what is the difference between a Boost and an Ad?

A boost is only for posts that you have added to your page. It could be anything – a link, a picture, etc. It is ideally a post that people find intriguing and has a high engagement factor, though you can boost a post right away. You can "boost" or pay to have that particular post get shown to more people.

When you boost you can choose the demographic and determine if you want more people who like your page to see it, or their friends, or even exclude those that like your page. This again, will be based upon your social media goals.

The major benefit of a boosted post is that you can wait until your exact target market has already voted on it! They have told you that this is something that is attracting them to the page and they want to see more of it. So, use Facebook's handy little reminders and hints to boost your posts and watch. Is it working? Good. If not, try again.

A Facebook ad on the other hand is a brand new post created for a specific purpose that has not been voted on by your fans already and is not usually posted on your page. The targeting is the same as a boost and setting the audience you desire is very similar. However, you can set a few more guidelines, create specific audiences and send your audience directly to another website when you create an ad versus a boost.

I use a combination of boosts and ads depending on my desired outcome. If I am trying to increase engagement on the page, then I will boost some well performing posts or posts that I want to be seen by more people such as blogs. I will then use ads for page likes, to compare results to a boost or to send people to a specific website.

One more aspect of your page that can truly benefit from ads – your events. Facebook allows you to boost your event to a specific target audience. You basically create an ad for your event and attract the correct demographic to your event page or to a specific call to action like signing up.

One client of mine runs classes monthly. They rotate and change each month depending on the season. Each class costs anywhere from $25 to $45. Every time he posts a class he will boost the event for $25 and since he started boosting them – he has filled his classes to capacity, making 5 to 10 times of his initial investment.

The Focus Platforms

–

No, you don't have to be on them all

"The successful warrior is the average man, with laser-like FOCUS." –Bruce Lee

The biggest decision when starting a digital strategy is to determine where you should be. What is the difference between each platform and how will they help to represent your brand?

Knowing each platforms' differences, matched with your Power of 5 strategy will help you to determine exactly where you should be online. Do you need to be on every platform? My answer is no. You need to be where your target demographic is.

I know that there are social media experts and agencies that will tell you that you need to be on every platform to reach everyone on the planet. Yet, if you are pitching to your niche, like you should be, then that is not only unnecessary, it is unrealistic for almost every small business and entrepreneur I know. If your plan is to one day have a full-time marketing department, then by all means, be present on every platform. Until then, pitch to your niche and stay where your target demographic is.

There are really four main platforms that you should choose from when you start your social media presence. Facebook, Instagram, LinkedIn and Twitter. They have been around the longest and currently, have the largest number of worldwide users.

Some folks aren't big fans of Facebook. My answer to that is that you haven't seen the power of their targeted ads if that is how you feel about it. For a small business marketer this platform is the stuff of dreams.

Is it perfect? No. But no other social media platform has convinced its users to share more information organically that can be used for extremely targeted ad campaigns.

Facebook has over 2 billion monthly active users as of the time of this writing. This is the largest amount of users on any social media platform and it only continues to grow year over year.

Out of those 2 billion monthly active users, there are 1.23 billion mobile daily active users. Do you need any other information to convince you that everything you do needs to be mobile friendly?

Another stat for you – Facebook has over 1.23 billion DAILY active users.

Why is this an important stat? Because it shows that not only does Facebook have a ton of people who use its platform, but that they use it daily and consistently. This loyalty from a fan base is exactly what you want when you are deciding where to market your product or business. But also remember, because they are consistent in their efforts, they expect the same from the pages they follow.

Facebook is a game of posting consistently. When an audience is on a platform daily, they expect the same from their fan pages. If you post once a week, maybe less, than you will not only lose the faith of your fans, but your reach will plummet.

Facebook rewards those that post often and pay to play. The algorithms can be beat, but you need to understand how they work before you can manipulate the rules. It is one of my favorite sayings – Know the rules, so that you know how to break them. I'm not sure who actually said that, but I was always the girl that wanted to constantly hit the red button, you know, the one that everyone constantly tells you not to push.

(Facebook stats from Facebook 2/1/17)

#SocialKEY – Know the rules, then BREAK them

Testing and measuring, playing with the limits and fighting to work outside the norm is what social media is all about. The rules of traditional marketing have been turned on its head. What worked yesterday is now obsolete. Try a new method and strategy – push your limits to break through.

Social media is all about finding new buttons to push on every platform. What works today may not work tomorrow. It is a game of constant refining and re-focus, which is often why my customers will come to me. Keeping up with your own industry is hard enough, trying to keep track of the daily changes on social media? Clearly, it is a career all in itself.

Instagram is Facebook's little brother. Literally – Facebook bought Instagram a few years back and have consistently worked to create algorithms and challenge the new platforms on the block like Snapchat. Instagram is the platform for your company if you present your products or services best through images. It can be a bit tricky to post since you can't schedule it to go automatically, but let's look at the stats.

There are 600 million monthly users and 400 million active daily users. 80% of these users are from outside the US, with 20% being approximately 78 million people. So, while it doesn't necessarily stack up to the behemoth that Facebook is, it is growing and powered by Facebook and their ads manager.

The ability to set up an ad campaign in Facebook and have it run on both platforms for one price, is invaluable for a small business on both platforms. The statistics you can glean let you know where you should be focusing your efforts and how to tweak your efforts on each platform.

There are two things that I wish were different about Instagram. It is not a click through site – meaning that you cannot link your posts to any website. You can put the URL in the comments or description, but those seeing the posts need to copy and paste it in their browser instead of a direct link. The only place to have a live link is on your profile summary. Therefore, if you have a blog you need to change that URL often. It isn't a deal breaker for most companies, but it does present a challenge that Pinterest does not have.

This however, is possibly changing. Just recently Instagram announced a new feature for retailers using Shopify that allows users to click to purchase. Excellent news for future possibilities.

The other aspect of Instagram that makes marketing on the platform a bit trickier is the inability to schedule a post for later publishing. Instagram only allows you to post from your phone. While you may be able to see the posts on your desktop, you have to have your phone in order to post the image. You can use additional tools, but they are not native to Instagram.

Twitter is a different beast from Facebook and Instagram. Every day it is a toss-up as to whether it will continue to fight and actually make a profit. As of this writing it is still struggling but everyone is paying attention to it. The current US President uses it so much that you would think he has saved it, but alas, that is not really the situation. I would argue that more people are paying attention to it because of President Trump, but the number of users has not drastically increased, nor has the profit for the company. Time will tell if this continues to be true.

Twitter* currently has 313 million monthly users with 79% of them being outside of the US. This is only slightly behind Instagram, yet this platform has a completely different demographic. Its recently updated 280 character posting limit, creates unique challenges and opportunities for companies when working to build relationships. It is a fast moving platform where you need to focus on the trending tweet of the day and get in on the conversations.
(*Twitter stats from Twitter.com)

So what type of company is Twitter best suited for? Personal coaches, entrepreneurs, small businesses, B2C focused companies and those that are focused on the daily news. Twitter literally has the pulse of what is trending in the world.

Each day when you bring it up there is a list of 5 to 10 trending topics. Add a hashtag to your post and get in on a conversation. Those that reach out will tell you that they can get a solid funnel of clients from Twitter.

This is an excellent sister platform for Facebook. You can send people to your Facebook account in a post or a DM. It is one of the few platforms where people are genuinely trying to connect with strangers. You don't see a lot of kids and puppy posts. This is somewhere where people go to share information and to attain it quickly. They will search for advice and help, while connecting with others who share the same interests.

The platform for business is LinkedIn. That being said, I don't love the LinkedIn business pages. I think that they are a total waste of time for many reasons, but the main reason is because LinkedIn is built on the idea of individuals connecting. It was designed as an online business networking and recruiting tool where individuals could go for new opportunities or to share their own openings. As an individual profile though, LinkedIn can be invaluable.

The goal on LinkedIn is to be active and present. The best times to post are in the morning, and usually in the middle of the week. The second-best times are around the lunch hour and about an hour before the end of the day. You want to post valuable content that your colleagues will want to read. Whether it is sharing a post from another site or writing one yourself on their publishing platform, the key is to make it relevant and useful.

LinkedIn can definitely be a place for inspirational images and the sharing of what is happening in the office, but remember it is more of a place to connect with other professionals. Always think of LinkedIn as a networking group. You want to know more about others than talk about you – so make sure you share insights of your industry and not just your business all the time. No one likes a constant braggart.

The last of the major platforms is YouTube.

This is where if you have information to share in video form – do it here.

Side Note - I am going to contradict myself here a bit. If you are on Facebook do what you can to keep your video native to Facebook. Post other content, longer content on YouTube. On pretty much any other platform a link to YouTube works just fine. But Facebook doesn't like you to play outside of its platform, so it will automatically boost a native video and let a YouTube one die. Not fair, I know, but true in many cases. Not all, but many.

YouTube has over a billion users. So out of all the platforms it is the only one rivaling Facebook in users. Every day people watch hundreds of millions of hours on YouTube.

Let that sink in – hundreds of millions.

This clearly generates billions of views. Its main demographic are those from 18 – 49 and more than half of people watch videos on their mobile.

(Stats from YouTube.com)

If you provide solid content, then people will watch for hours. However, you need to catch someone within the first minute to hook them. I won't watch a video much longer than 10 minutes, but my husband will be on there for hours for a video that catches his interest. This leads squarely back to who is your target demographic.

This platform also lets you monetize your videos. This is excellent if you are creating consistent, valuable content. This is not a quick income generator. It can take some time, yet again, if you are consistent and build a strong following, it can be a fantastic revenue stream.

The runner-up platforms are Pinterest, Snapchat and Houzz.

Pinterest is a platform based on images. Therefore, if your company is on Instagram, once you have nailed it there, you should expand to Pinterest. There are 150 million active users on Pinterest with 60% female and 40% male. One surprising fact is that Millennials now make up 67% of users and for many online shoppers (55%) Pinterest is their favorite social media platform.

(Facts from expandedramblings.com and Pinterst.com 2/2017)

There are a lot of bonuses to being on Pinterest. One of them being that Pinterest is a click through site.

You can make every pin forward to a website once someone clicks it. So, if it is not pointing straight back to your website then you can make that happen. Obviously, you wouldn't change an article destination, or mess with a link of some content that you did not create. The ability to change the source URL or destination website after you click it can blur the lines of ethics for some.

Pinterest also doesn't require much interaction, but it does require pinning. You need to be consistent with pinning daily. This is where one of those pinning programs that will seek pins for you based on your boards and interests can be helpful if you aren't pinning your own content daily, or don't have enough of it to pin.

What is enough? Ten to twenty pins a day will keep your account active, but with Pinterest, more is better. It allows you to reach your demographic and stay top of mind with your followers by having Pinterest suggest your new pins when someone opens their feed. And don't worry about having every pin relate to your exact subject. Some of the best Pinterest boards for companies are simple, like the color of their brand. Love hot pink? Make it a board. Redoing your kitchen? Make it a board. People flock to those with like interests. It is the PERSON behind the pinning that people are following. That is actually true for any platform, but that's another chapter.

Snapchat is a newer platform where up until now it may not make sense for a business to jump on the bandwagon. They have 158 million daily users and 301 million active monthly users. There are 2.5 billion snaps sent per day. Yes, billion with a B.

(Facts from expandedramblings.com)

They have recently introduced a search function which allows people to find trending topics and other hot stories, where that was not an option previously. If you didn't know that persons name on Snapchat then you couldn't find them. It looks like they are working to refine their features because Facebook is gunning for them. They are also in the midst of a redesign and a reboot – working to gain market share in a social media world they never really planned to enter. They originally were a simple messaging app – more like Facebook Messenger. Now, they are working to compete for ad dollars and having a challenging time in the race.

Who is Snapchat for? I'm glad you asked.

Snapchat is a platform designed for younger audiences – teenagers and early twenties are the dominating force. Yes, there are some older demographics, but the number of younger users far outweighs the number of older ones.

Is that your target demographic? The other question when determining if Snapchat is ideal for your business, is how often can you create organic, in the moment stories? Do you love video? Then it may be the perfect platform for you. This is not ideally a platform you have hired out by some other company to do. You need to be present and active on this platform, with your company's spokesperson as the shining star.

We also have Houzz. If you have never heard of Houzz then you haven't had to do a home remodel or build in the past few years. This platform was created by a couple who wanted gorgeous images to browse through when they were redoing their home from multiple contractors, designers, builders, etc. There are 40 million active users on the platform with 25 million unique visitors every month. There are over 4 million photos and over 3 million products for sale on Houzz as well.

(Facts from expandedramblings.com)

If you are in the business of dealing with home restoration, renovation or remodels, then you should have a profile on Houzz. This is where you highlight your best projects, but interaction is key to really gaining clients on Houzz. They have an entire section for prospective clients to ask design dilemma problems and every time you post an image, anyone can ask you for the color of the paint to the type of flooring you used. You need to be prompt in replying and answer with the idea that even if this person may not be your ideal customer, your reply to their comment could be seen by your ideal demographic and how you respond could be what makes them pick up the phone.

Houzz does have what they call the Pro plan. Every client that I have worked with has not found value in this plan. It costs a lot of money for very little return. You can get just as much exposure on the site by uploading images to your ideabooks weekly and answering questions for users on a bi-weekly basis. I am sure that there are some businesses that have benefited greatly from the plan, but I haven't found any of them.

#SocialExperience

A client recently shared with me that they don't work regularly on Houzz anymore because Houzz has decided to sell their own products online, basically cutting out the designer who may have that item in their warehouse. This is in direct competition to many businesses and they have felt betrayed. For the consumer it is a win, yet something to think about when you begin your Houzz profile. Do you sell products? I would highlight your expertise instead. People buy from people – if they like you and your business because you have been helpful and informative, they will buy from you and not Houzz.

While I was writing this book a brand new platform popped up which could be a game changer for many businesses who sell products on Amazon. It is called Amazon Spark. Amazon

Spark is currently only available for Prime members and you need to spend a minimum amount on Amazon to qualify. Lucky for you, I do and so I was able to get a sneak peek on this brand new platform.

It is a merging of what many love about Instagram and Pinterest. It allows you to post images of what you are doing or loving at the moment with the added bonus of being able to buy what you see in the picture – right then and there with the click of a button. This is an online shopper's paradise.

When you open your account you choose from multiple different interests (women's fashions, toys and games, books, etc) and are shown a feed from others who are posting about these interests. These interests are directly related to the sales categories on Amazon. I was trying to search for a broad Kids interest and it wasn't there, but babies or toys and games, was ready for me to choose.

This platform was built with two things in mind – the Influencers of the digital world and people who love instant gratification. I'm not lying, I wanted to purchase an adorable Coach purse last night after only being on the app for less than ten minutes. This could be excellent for those selling products on Amazon, possibly bad for my pocketbook. This is exactly what we want from a social media platform, something set up with a specific purpose – you know Amazon is trying to sell you something, so you expect it – and delivers actual clients and customers.

There are paid posts denoted by the #sponsor note that tells you when someone is advertising, yet it is just another picture – there are no words on the images as of now and you barely know it's a sponsored post. All of the posts, whether sponsored or not, if they have an item or one similar that they sell on Amazon it is highlighted by a small shopping bag and dots on the picture that pop up once you click on it.

This has the capacity to be HUGE but it could also die quickly like a number of other platforms come and gone. But since Amazon powers this one, I'm going to bet on a successful run and large growth potential.

Are there additional platforms out there? Of course. There is Tumbler and Medium for bloggers, Google Plus, and multiple other small ones that are working to be the next Facebook.

Medium is excellent for additional exposure for your blog, but it's not necessarily as well-known so it makes a great extra avenue for those playing in the blogospere or testing out new content. Tumbler has been around since 2007 and has a massive blog – over 280 million to be exact. If you are blogging – this is another space to play in.

Google Plus is like the red headed stepchild of the social media world. You have some people that swear by the platform and absolutely love it and then you have the other side of the spectrum where it is useless and only one more way for Google to gain information about you for search results. I tend to lean on the latter end of the spectrum.

The only reason I recommend to my clients that they have a Google plus page is so that Google will help them to be found quicker. Google scans Google sites, so ensuring your business is seen and has a space here is important for search rankings. But don't worry about posting, unless you love it, then by all means, go for it.

Words have power.
TV has power.
My pen has power.
- Shonda Rhimes

Establish Yourself as the Expert

"Life isn't about trying to be an expert in everything. It's about being an expert in one thing and offering it to the world." – Bo Sanchez

Social media gives you a unique advantage – you can establish yourself as an expert in your field so that others will come to find you. This is a main key in attraction marketing.

Do you need a blog? Yes.

Does it have to be a written blog? No.

Some people can write, and others are great on video. Where are your strengths and what are you the most comfortable with? That is the way you need to go.

Why do you need a blog?

I'm so glad you asked.

Blogging is the key item for establishing yourself as an expert in your field. It allows you to share with others what you know and why you know it. It doesn't matter if it's written or on video, what matters is that you publish it consistently and contain solid information for your target market. This is your Power 5. Who do you want to read your blog? Create it for them.

Remember, you are not alienating others if you narrow in on your target market; you are defining who you are. Does it really matter if you have someone who doesn't like your company? NO, that just means that there is more room for those that do.

So, this blog...where do you publish it?

You need to have it on your website for multiple reasons. One is to create links back to your company's page and showcase there that you do know what you are doing. The second reason is that it helps with your Google search results.

Google will scan websites with its fancy algorithms on a constant basis. If your website stays static, then it will stop scrolling yours. Yet if your site is consistently updated and linked to other sites (when you share on social) then Google will work its magic and refresh your site within its search results, usually pushing you up higher on the search results page.

Besides your website you need to post your blog on your social media platforms. If you choose to do a video blog, then I actually suggest posting it to YouTube and then sharing that link to your website. This allows you to benefit from the search tools on YouTube and will send more people to your site without a lot of work from you. This also allows you to avoid putting large files on your website, since the video will technically be hosted on YouTube.

In the case of both a written and video blog, once it is on your website – you need to post it to every social media platform you are on. Facebook, Twitter, Pinterest, LinkedIn, and Google+ (if its still around...there is debate on this one but that's another book altogether).

If it is a written blog, you can also publish it within blogging sites such as Medium and use LinkedIn's publishing feature. Often social media platforms will boost things written natively within their site more than just a link from a website.

> **#SocialKEY: Don't make all your posts the same on every platform.**
>
> Every post, especially if it's the same article or blog, needs to have different content to describe the link that is tailored to that platform.

Now – here is the real trick when you post a blog to all your sites. You don't want the posts to be the same. Every post on each one of your sites should be tailored to your customers on that platform. The tagline for Facebook should be different than that on Twitter, Pinterest, LinkedIn and so on. Each one should have a different picture when it is posted and formatted for the correct platform.

This allows you to post it multiple times during your publishing window. On Twitter you would never post it just once. Set up a blast with every blog, to go out every day with a unique message each time. You should look at every platform and see how often you can or should post it. Maybe you post it once on Facebook but then boost it to see what traction you bring to your page instead of posting it multiple times a week.

Then you test and measure.

One post of the blog may fail miserably, another could go viral and still another could get solid engagement but never be shared. You never know what may happen or know what phrase will resonate with your clients more than others. This is why you have to constantly monitor what you are doing online and ensure that not only your message is consistent, but that it is hitting the emotional pressure points of your target audience. If it isn't going well, then re-post and try again!

The wonder of social media is that anything can be deleted and everything can be re-posted at a different time to attract a new market. Multiple pages and accounts have been re-launched by marketers around the world who are on a constant search of that one post that will go viral.

There are no secrets to success.
It is the result of preparation,
hard work, and learning from failure.
- Colin Powell

Unicorn Hunting
The Viral Post Every
Marketer Dreams Of

"Believe that there ARE Unicorns." – Shakespeare

This is the Holy Grail to all social media marketers. A post that you have created has been shared hundreds, thousands, even a million times.

And it is an elusive prize.

You never know when a post will go viral or why it might resonate more than a different one that you had published with what you think is the same thought process. Yet there is one thing that all viral posts have in common – it hits some emotional button with people.

There is something called Maslow's Hierarchy of Needs.

This basically lays out every emotional need we have as humans and the real skill of every marketer is crafting your message so that it hits one of these buttons.

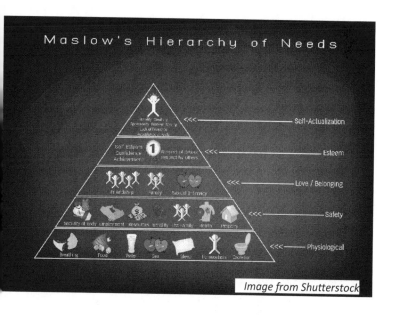

McDonald's may be one of the greatest marketing machines on earth. Each commercial they have is unique and targeted for a specific niche and they are run on television according to the time those prospective customers may be watching.

There are commercials focused on the elderly and their feelings of belonging to a similar community with early morning coffee. A mom and her kids with happy meals, twenty somethings going for coffee with their friends and high school kids getting a meal after practice – there is something for everyone and each one pulls on similar emotions. Feeling like you belong in a happy gathering place where everyone is sharing something together. Whether you like the food or not, their messaging is something to envy and emulate.

The question is – how do you take this type of emotion and transfer it to social media? Clients will tell me – it's easy to tell a story with a commercial but when you transfer that same thought process to social media it can get lost. And they are right – it can.

There is a system on social media that works to effectively tell your story and its called bread-crumbing. Or what I like to call the Hansel and Gretel method of advertising. (If you don't know who Hansel and Gretel are then please take a moment and Google it. I can wait...Got it? Good.)

This method basically allows you to share a small piece of your story every day. It is how to slowly reveal an overall strategy to people in such a way that they want to come back every day and see what you will be posting next. Because that's something else that prospective clients and customers want – more.

When you hook them with a story, when they latch on to some emotional pull that you have provided, they will come back day after day to look for your next post. They will come back to see how your story will unfold.

An example of using the Hansel and Gretel method would look something like this for a fitness brand focused on new moms.

Post 1: Post a picture of a pregnant mom with something about how exciting it is to be a new mom. Are you ready for your little miracle?

Post 2: Post an image of a slightly sleep deprived mom – little miracles can keep us up at night

Post 3: Post an image of a baby sleeping and mom doing Yoga – we all need OUR time

Post 4: Post about your new fitness group focused specifically on new moms who are ready to take back their fitness and provide calm in the storm of raising a new baby

Post 5: Post a collage image of mom working out then/feeding baby/mom having coffee – saying something like fitness puts the balance back in life and adds a routine to the daily chaos with a new baby

Another example may be for a plumbing company.

Post 1: Water exploding

Post 2: Mom making a phone call being sprayed by said pipe bursting

Post 3: Plumber responding to the call with a pic of a clock showing little time has passed

Post 4: Water pipe being fixed while children run around and mom in background

Post 5: Mom thanking plumber and seeing him or her out the door

Each example could easily be done in one commercial or video, but they can also be shown in images and slowly fed into the feed of any social platform. In between those posts you can add articles that you have written or even an inspirational image focused on your target demographic.

Taking a small piece of a campaign and drip-feeding it to your audience is one of the best ways to share a story and bring your audience into your business. Stories pull on our emotional strings more than anything else. We can relate to stories because at some point in our lives either that same thing has happened to us, a friend or relative or we can see it happening and envision ourselves in that situation.

This method is also excellent for sharing personal stories. One day giving a crumb about your history, the next about your vision, then how you started to move forward, then a looking back post, another about a major success, then another success, maybe followed by a failure.

Think about what it is that you want to share with your prospective clients and customers and then chop it up into little pieces. Those pieces are what you share.

Crafting your story and determining the message you want to share with your prospects is one of the most important and most difficult pieces of any digital strategy. This is because we are often so focused on ourselves that we fail to think of our customers.

I was in retail for a very long time and there is a sales adage that was repeated daily – features tell, benefits sell. It's not what you do, it's what you can do for a customer. How your service can benefit them in some way that people want to know.

Everyone has a story. Every company has a benefit to their customers that they can't quite see. This is where my team and I come in. We help to craft your story and then share it with the world piece by piece in just the right order.

#SocialFAIL: You give your whole story away at once.

When I started telling my own story online I would word vomit all over a post. It would be long and intense and hardly *anyone* (read only family and MAYBE a friend or two because I would ask them to) would read the whole thing. As a culture we are conditioned to read less and less at a time. We like bullet points and quick 140 character sentences. The fast-paced world is also creating attention spans that are constantly getting shorter. Posting really long stories loses most of your message.

Keep it short. Keep it on message. Add a picture.

We don't learn from talking;
we learn from LISTENING.

Protect and Improve Your Online Reputation – Listen to the Voices

"Your brand isn't what you say it is, it's what Google says it is." – Chris Anderson

There are three main actions that you must take for social media success – Posting, Engagement and Listening. The last one may be one of the most important. One bad tweet, one horrible review or ugly post on Facebook can literally drop a stock price faster than anything else in today's digital world.

The reason? Because information travels much faster than it ever did before.

As United Airlines can attest – within hours of a poor customer service action by your staff, it can be shared millions of times on multiple continents. On April 9, 2017 Chicago Aviation officers dragged a Chinese doctor off a United Airlines plane because his seat was going to be given to a United Airlines Flight crew due to the flight being overbooked. This particular gentleman was due back to work in his hospital in Kentucky the next day and was not going to volunteer to give up his seat.

This fiasco was recorded by multiple passengers and then promptly posted to just about every social networking platform available. Within minutes it was shared and people began to demand answers. How could this happen? Why would this happen? A woman walked off the plane with children because she stated that they shouldn't have to see this.

The flight crew was unapologetic. The social stratosphere was on fire – and all of this publicity was damaging United's credibility and showing how poor their customer service was. To make matters worse, United was just about to expand to China and this situation certainly didn't win any fans there.

Immediately people started to call for the flight crew to be fired, for the CEO to resign or change the rules and everyone was waiting for the stock to tank. The CEO quickly made the situation much worse by supporting his crew and refusing to apologize to the doctor, turning one horrible incident into a public relations nightmare.

The CEO has since offered another two apologies, appeared on morning talk shows and finally changed the rules for overbooking. Within hours this company had alienated millions of potential customers and possibly threatened their expansion into China because of one horrible situation.

Before social media, this may have gone unnoticed. You may have had this spread to 100 people, those on the plane and their friends, but never to this degree.

Have you Googled yourself lately? Take a minute and do it now. Really, put down this book and type in your name and then the name of your business.

Now search for every version of your name – if you have a company name with a number in it then search for the number spelled out and then using the number. IE: 5guys, Five Guys, five_guys, five-guys, 5-guys, 5_guys, 5 guys, etc

Do you know what will come up? People will make their decisions based on what they find online.

Does this surprise you?

During a networking presentation that I attended just a couple of months ago they had what they were calling An Interview with a Millennial. The Millennial being interviewed was asked a question from the audience that left most of the attendees speechless. She was asked "If you were to get information from the expert in that field or business versus an opinion from a friend or review from a stranger on Facebook or other form of digital media – which would you trust more?

Her answer that had most of the room stunned?

Her friend or complete strangers review on social media.

Think about that for just one minute.

Your opinion about how great your business is and how fantastic you are at your career is close to meaningless to this Millennial and many others like her. This is one of the largest demographics that are starting to truly make an impact on the economy. What is the first thing they do whenever they encounter a business? Google it.

The second thing? They reach out to friends on social media to figure out if it is a worthy place to go. This is one of the reasons that I instruct my clients to get as many online reviews as humanly possible. Facebook and Google reviews are extremely important in the review space.

A note here on Yelp. Many people will tell you that a positive review is excellent and that bad reviews can really have a negative impact on your business...and they would be right. Yet there have been rumors that Yelp does something awful and they have been caught.

They try to blackmail or as one judge called it "hard bargaining but not extortion" many businesses. They will call you non-stop to join their special programs and basically threaten that if a bad review comes along that they can't do anything about it. But if you are a paying customer they can bury your negative reviews.

Sounds like it may be beneficial at first...but then it became apparent that not all the reviews from Yelp were authentic. To my knowledge Yelp has worked to change their practices, after multiple lawsuits, but if you have to pay for a review then I think it's a bad call.

Another thing about reviews is that even a bad review can be good for a business if it is handled in a good way. For example, if someone writes about your poor customer service – take the time to respond to them and offer then some sort of apology and discount for a future service. Others will see your reply and that you are taking the steps to improve your service and that will bring in new clients.

So how do you get these very important reviews? Go and ask!

So often people won't ask their best clients for a review. If these clients love your work, then they will happily help to spread the word. However, if you don't ask, then they may or may not even think to write a review for you.

Not only should you go and ask your best clients right now, but then after each service call or interaction with a client, ask them to write a review for you. Often your business will grow exponentially based on the feedback from your clients and this is where the magic happens. That Millennial who trusts a review more than you? They will see that, refer you to their friends, even if they haven't used your services themselves, and your organic traffic will grow.

The Power of a Facebook Like - Hint: It's Not that Powerful

"If you just set out to be liked, you would be prepared to compromise on anything at any time, and you would achieve NOTHING." – Margaret Thatcher

There are some massive misconceptions about a Like on Facebook. Most people's first reaction to someone liking their Facebook business page is pride, happiness, excitement even. "Someone liked my page! Yes, I am clearly doing something right."

Well…yes and no.

The truth is that you can have hundreds, thousands and perhaps millions of fans (those people who have liked your page) but only a very small percentage will see any of your posts in their newsfeed. When I say small, I mean very small - as in two to four percent of your fans.

I can hear you screaming right now – What? Why do I even post then? We will get to that, but first here are the reasons why it is that small, and how we combat it.

One is the algorithm that Facebook uses to determine a post's popularity. Within the first few minutes that you post something to your page, Facebook begins to track it. If someone "engages" with your post, meaning they Like, Comment or Share it, then Facebook will continue to deliver it into your fans newsfeed. People vote, and it continues to be seen. This is where you get your reach number that is on every single post.

Yet there is something that your fans don't know. If they like your page and don't like any of the posts on your page...they will more than likely never see your posts.

Let that sink in for just a minute.

Someone likes your page. They assume they will see your posts. Then they wonder why they never do, or worse, assume that you don't post anything worth seeing.

This is why only two to four percent of your fans see your posts. It is also why Facebook pushes you to boost your posts. In order to reach everyone who likes your page, and possibly their friends, you need to pay to play.

So how do you combat this? Two ways. Inform your fans – make an excellent graphic and pin it to the top of your page. *Like my page? Make sure*

*you like your favorite post for more of that content
if you want to see it in your newsfeed!*

And the other option – pay for it. Boosting posts
and running ads is one of the best tools from
Facebook. They may have an algorithm that you
need to figure out a work around for, but when
you consider their highly targeted ad options,
done correctly, it is worth the money every time.

This is the exact reason why I tell all my clients
that it's not always about how many likes you
have on your page. It's how many engagements
your posts receive, how many people ask you
questions, or click your call to action button.
Every single business has a different need based
on their business priorities. This is often where I
help my clients out. Based on your business goals
we determine a digital strategy to help you get
the biggest bang for your investment, in money
and time.

For example, I have a client that is a preschool. Their number one goal was to have their student's parents be more engaged on their page. This singular focus meant that we weren't going after likes on the page, but working to increase comments, likes and shares of individual posts.

Our singular strategy led to some amazing results after only one year of consistency.

Within one week of opening their enrollment to the public for the next year they had filled all of their morning spots. This was faster than any other year in their 16-year history. They also have a significant wait list for their summer camps and have had more action on their Facebook page than ever before. We have never run an ad campaign, yet we have prompted parents to get involved. Interacted with other pages and shared valuable information about our school and events for the family. This is the power of being social.

What about the other social media platforms? Do they all run on algorithms? No, but the truly important question that you need to ask is "What platforms are my clients on"? This is the single most important question any business can ask to run a solid digital strategy.

> **#SocialKEY: Be where your customers are.**
>
> Each demographic prefers one social media platform over the other. Home in on your niche and if you are only on one platform, make sure it's where your prospective clients are.

Content is KING but
Engagement is QUEEN
and she rules the house!
- Mari Smith

Creating Clients and Customers with Groups

"If you make a sale, you can make a living. If you make an investment of time and good service in a customer, you can make a fortune." – Jim Rohn

Groups are hidden gems on social media. Almost every platform has a way to gather a group of individuals and allow them to speak about a single common interest. Facebook has their groups – secret, closed or public, Twitter has the ability to have lists and twitter parties surrounding a similar hashtag, LinkedIn has its groups and Pinterest has shared boards.

Groups give us a safe place to speak to others that are like us. They share a common interest and it is often those interests that allow us to make stronger business and personal connections.

Groups are the best place to begin to build relationships.

Social media is not a quick fix for any business. I can repeat this until I am blue in the face – this is a LONG GAME. 30 days will get you bupkis on social. It takes time to build solid relationships with those interested in your business and groups are the best place to begin to build. Start conversations by commenting on their thread, answering a question and being social.

This is also where you can get into trouble – don't do the sales thing. We are born salesmen. It's truly in our DNA. Watch any toddler work a room for something they want and then tell me that we weren't born to sell.

Yet, have you ever watched how they do it? They are relentless! Often its pure persistence - asking over and over for what they want, regardless of how many times you may say no. Yet when you are working to build relationships online (and really in life) it should be more about the other person than you – don't be the toddler in the room.

Don't tell them that they need to contact you right away. Ask questions, truly join the conversation. It is usually after the third or even fifth interaction with someone that they might find out what I do for a living.

Give more than you expect in return. Answer questions without thinking about what will come back to you and position yourself as someone who is willing to help versus just talk about themselves. This is so important in groups because you can easily become blacklisted. Talk too much about your business and you will be blocked. Come off as sleazy with no interest in the group members and you will be kicked out.

Facebook has recently updated their groups and how they interact with their business pages. Something that business marketers have been dying to have – a business page can now link to a group and interact (comment and like) AS YOUR PAGE.

THIS IS HUGE. Why? Because previously you had to go in as your personal Facebook profile and speak to prospective clients. Now you can create groups that are formed from your own page and interact and attract potential clients.

For example: I have a fitness page (FITSISTERS) that runs monthly fitness motivation groups. Previously we had to interact as our individual profiles, but now we can act as our page, constantly promoting our page and our daily posts.

Another client is a company that hosts networking groups. Now they can connect and post daily to keep the conversations focused and the group useful to its users. As a Facebook page you can now create any group that will benefit your business. Are you a business coach? Form a group for budding entrepreneurs. Kids crafts or a local tradesman? Mom groups are gold, I know, I'm in at least two of them. MLM? Create a group based on your shared interests from your power 5.

Facebook isn't the only platform where groups are an important part of attracting the right market. On LinkedIn, groups are often your bread and butter. When you join a group it expands your network and gives you access to the hundreds or thousands of members in the group. As a business it can also be a gateway to something much more.

Social Media Examiner is a website that does a blog, podcast, social media marketer networking events and now they have what they are calling the Social Media Marketing Society. I am a huge fan of Michael Steltzner and everything they do at SME. How did I find out about them? I was in their LinkedIn group for social media marketers.

The group often had conversations started by the admins and discussions were rampant. Then they had a brilliant idea – they monetized it. They took their group to new levels by taking it to a paid group. Then they went one step more – they have launched the Social Media Marketing Society where they will have discussions and trainings. They slowly built a group of dedicated individuals by providing valuable content and priceless trainings, and have now monetized it. Brilliant.

Our groups on FITSISTERS are also where we recruit and attract clients. We have a simple fitness motivation group where we all post to attract new perspective clients and then specific groups where we have our paying clients who get one on one attention.

Twitter has lists and the ability to have hashtag parties. Lists are something where you basically group together a bunch of people that you follow who have common interests. Other people can look at lists that are set to public and you often want to label them as something complimentary to those in the lists. For example someone put me on a list called Beautiful Moms. I can tell you that I was extremely humbled and flattered when that happened. Its just a simple list with moms on Twitter, but calling it Beautiful Moms made me want to check out the owner of this list and ensure that I looked at the group they had added me too. What types of lists can you create that your core audience would find valuable?

Remember, every single move you make on social media is to attract your core demographic. You may love the show NCIS, but is that something your key demographic loves? Does it really have anything to do with your business? This is the difference between followers and fans and clients and customers. When you ensure that your actions are truly focused on your target audience you are attracting future business, not just another stat.

#SocialFAIL: Using your Business Page like your Personal Page

Keep it professional. I enjoy a funny mom post from time to time, but if it doesn't appeal to my niche market, then it doesn't go anywhere near my business page. Keep to your focused areas to ensure you are attracting your key market. If it's not working then change it up, but be wary about posting random things on your page with no purpose consistently. Your posts can then get confusing and your message will be lost.

I mentioned hashtag parties. This is where you make an announcement that you will be live on Twitter for a certain amount of time for a specific purpose. Those that want to speak to you need to use a specific hashtag to get your attention. Sometimes if a Twitter party is particularly successful you can turn that hashtag and those that interacted with you into a list as well.

As for Pinterest – having a shared board allows you to attract others that you think may be interested in your product or service. The board doesn't need to necessarily be directly related to your brand, but something that will bring the ideal client.

I have a client who owns a custom stair building business. We have designed boards based on seasonal weddings where they use stairs in the wedding in some way. This would be an excellent board to share with photographers, florists and anyone else who may be interested in this demographic. Sharing this type of board with other professionals is an immediate way to gain followers from other businesses that may have similar interests. It is also an excellent way to attract businesses to work with you on joint projects or as a source for referrals.

People do not buy goods and services,
they buy relations, stories and magic.
- Seth Godin

Influencer Marketing – Yes, Mommy Bloggers Have Taken Over the World

"People do not buy goods and services. They buy relations, stories and magic."
– Seth Godin

Today it is possible for anyone to be an influencer. It takes time and consistent effort – but if you are focused on your niche and know what you are talking about, then you can create a massive amount of power online.

What is an influencer? Anyone online with a massive amount of followers on one or multiple platforms. When I say massive, we are talking about millions of followers. You can also be a micro-influencer, with less followers, but the main appeal of an influencer in the social media world is that the people who follow them are active and moved to take action based on their advice.

There are influencers in every single industry you can imagine and on every platform. Not all YouTube influencers have a Facebook presence and not all Instagrammers have a presence anywhere else. They are often unique to their platform, yet one thing remains the same, they are considered experts in their field and have amassed a huge amount of influence on the online community at large.

Mommy bloggers are usually top of mind – Scary Mommy is one such blog who was started by a stay at home mom to chronicle her day-to-day life at home with her kids. That was in 2008. As of 2015 her blog and her online persona were purchased by a media company (Some Spider) who continues with similar content to Jill's and much more.

I know that there are many women out there that have no idea that Jill no longer owns and runs her own blog. Because I didn't until just this minute. I never thought to look at the about us and wonder if she had sold her blog – I love reading her articles and assumed they were still her. She still has influence a full year and a half after selling her blog.

Take a minute and think about this...

An everyday stay at home mom began a blog and for years companies were sending her products to try and asking her to give her opinion because they knew that her audience would be listening. And then she monetized it.

How do you find these influencers in your field? Google it. Seriously.

There are magazines that write articles on influencers in different industries all the time, because they do change. Influencers not only have a large online following, but they are people you have more than likely heard of through your own reading and research. Who do you go to online for greater awareness in your field?

Social media has a large number of influencers – from people who started out at Apple (Guy Kawasaki), fitness gurus turned business pros (Chalene Johnson), Facebook focused (Mari Smith) and so much more. There are social media agencies such as Hubspot that have proven their expertise in the field and the likes of Social M's, but it certainly doesn't stop with social media.

Some are influencers because they are already famous from their acting in movies or their television careers. But MOST influencers are sought out because they have an excellent blog or online presence on some platform, where they can share with their followers what product they are trying today.

How do you work with an influencer? Or better yet – how do you get their attention? You start SLOW. You build a relationship. Think of it as a courtship. Don't just send an email or shoot them a message on a platform saying – hey do you want to try my product? If they are a solid influencer, then they are getting this type of request daily and if you are a small start-up – they are not going to even acknowledge your message if it is a solid ask.

Think about how you would like to be romanced. What does the influencer get from you? Do you have a large following? Would they benefit from you sharing their information to your fan or follower base? Could you create a collaboration of some sort? Have you shared their blog or tweeted out a link that shows that you appreciate their content?

Attracting and building a relationship with an influencer is a courtship.

Rarely does anything happen on social media that takes a small amount of effort. It is a consistent process of searching for the right person to share your brand. Offering something that may be of value to them – sharing of information, collaborating with them on a blog, something that is going to somehow benefit them more than you.

In the beginning it is ALL about the influencer, not about you or your business. Once you have created a relationship with someone, then you can ask for something for you. But that is step three or 30 depending on the person, certainly not step one or two.

Influencer marketing has become so popular that Amazon has gotten on the bandwagon. They

163

have begun influencer pages for popular bloggers to actually sell the products they promote on Amazon with some sort of a percentage going to the influencer. This was a recent introduction in March of 2017. So while it is still new, it has already gotten some traction.

There is a word of warning with the influencer marketing process. Influencers are people and should be treated with kindness and respect for their status as influencers. Shooting out random message en mass, as I've seen some programs advertising to do, is not the way to anyone's heart.

Can you do that? Sure. Will you get results? Probably not.

Remember – how would you like to be treated? Because that's how you should approach any type of relationship with an influencer.

So, you have partnered with an influencer – now what?

Once you have made relationships with influencers in your industry the fun begins. You can send them products to review and post about to their following while you share it to your platforms. You can collaborate on a blog or interview them on a video where they may mention your service or product, or you may be able to get them to be a sponsor and part of a promotional strategy or campaign.

The point is to establish relationships with multiple influencers and then to capitalize on their influence by working to a mutually beneficial goal – selling more products with them benefiting in some way as well.

Some influencers want to get paid for product promotion, others want more exposure; it really depends on the person, their platform and their business goals. Once you have a relationship you will know what it is they want and position yourself and your company, to give it to them while benefiting from their influence on your market.

#SocialKEY:
Never underestimate the power of a good review.

Whether it is from an influencer or from your last customer – it should be shouted from the rooftops. Create an image with a key point from that review and say thank you. Not everyone will read a review, just like not everyone will be on the same platform as an influencer, so when you get the opportunity to share the positive thoughts from someone who has benefited from your service – DO IT!

Give ordinary people the right tools,
and they will design and build
the most extraordinary things.
- Neil Gershenfeld

Your Social Media Toolbox

"Learning with technology is a bit like carpentry. It's important to find the right tool for the job." – Mark Anderson

There is a rather large collection of tools available to you to help make running your social media a bit easier. There are scheduling tools to help ensure you are posting each day, curation tools to find the best relevant posts, even tools to help you un-follow other's on Twitter without ever having to go into your Twitter users.

The following is by no means an exhaustive list of every social media scheduling platform or app that can be used to help with your social media presence, but they are the ones I use the most and have had a great success with in managing my clients and my own businesses online.

The Schedulers & Monitors

Scheduling platforms are designed to do a bit of everything. They schedule posts, monitor your posts engagement, help to find relevant content to repost, give you a glimpse into your newsfeed on some platforms and allow you to search and engage in conversations - all while watching to see if people are talking about you through their mention features.

Hootsuite, Buffer, Social Sprout, Facebook Business Manager and Hubspot are the top main tools that come to mind for small businesses. I personally use Hootsuite and Facebook Business Manager to schedule and monitor my client's accounts because they are the easiest tool for me, and I've been through a trial with all of the above.

I'm a visual learner so Hootsuite matches my style. It is a maze of columns and images that allow me to track mentions, interact with others, follow people on Twitter and search for relevant articles or images to share with my followers or fans. It can also be extremely intimidating for many people.

I have one client who began on Buffer and is very happy with it. It schedules his posts and that is all he needs. This tool is also very good at allowing you to repost items you have had in the past and helps you to find relevant articles that have already been tweeted or posted on platforms as well. Hootsuite does this as well, but I have found that Buffer is just a little bit better.

Many people love Social Sprout due to their batch upload features. If you are creating large campaigns and want to post a huge amount of info, Hootsuite and Social Sprout tend to be the strongest contenders.

For those who are seeking the granddaddy of all social media management platforms – that is Hubspot. This tool has everything and anything you may ever need. From a scheduler to reports and analytics, this is an impressive tool. It is however, out of reach from a cost stand point for most of my small business clients and entrepreneurs. Nevertheless, it is an excellent resource for great blogs on social and business overall, if not ideal for your social media purposes.

#SocialKEY: A note on scheduling Facebook posts.

Facebook loves to have you stay within Facebook. If it could, I think it would have eliminated the ability for you to get out of Facebook when you are in the platform, but thankfully they can't hold us in Facebook land forever.

That being said, Facebook allows you to schedule your own posts right on your Facebook page. If this is the only platform you use, then it is an excellent tool and can give you great insight. I have found that some posts will even get greater traction if scheduled within Facebook, but that really depends on a variety of circumstances.

Facebook also has a tool for management of your page besides just your personal Facebook page - Business Manager. This tool was basically designed for businesses so that they could keep their business pages separate from their personal pages.

There is A LOT of discrepancy out there about whether it is bad, good or otherwise. I personally, find it very helpful to keep focused and get a quick snapshot of all of my pages stats, while also being able to have multiple ad accounts for each page. It keeps your personal messenger closed down and eliminates many of the distractions that may come with trying to focus on just your pages. It also allows you to put team members on your accounts without having to become friends with a colleague.

That is usually a big no-no for many people, they don't want to connect personally, they want to keep it professional – this tool allows you to do that. It can be seen as a complicated tool, but if you have more than one page, the ability to have multiple ad accounts and team assignments makes it worth the effort to learn it. You can always take your pages out, but you may find that the few shortcomings are not outweighed by the gains. If you only have one business Facebook page, then it may not be necessary unless you feel you need some of its specific features for ads or team members.

All of these tools have the ability to check analytics, monitor feedback and schedule your posts. I wanted something simpler for my clients and me. I wanted a tool that allowed you to schedule your posts and then, if you needed to reuse the same type of posts a year later – you could do that. I also wanted a scheduler that allowed my clients to preview, edit and approve the posts that my team was creating in one place versus using Facebook or Hootsuite for posts and Dropbox for images. This search led me to one conclusion – this tool didn't exist.

So I created it.

Social Labyrinth is a simple social media scheduling tool that will be launching in the spring of 2018. This tool is extremely simple in look and functionality. You won't find analytics because I feel that you can get the needed ones from the social media platforms or a variety of other tools on the market. You won't find mentions because again, those are in your notifications from your platforms. You can't track hashtags because you are scheduling out days or weeks in advance, not in the moment. You should be on your platforms daily and sometimes a scheduler gives you the false impression that you don't have to be.

What Social Labyrinth is - is a tool that allows you to schedule your posts, create campaigns for use now and in the future and something that will allow others, team members or clients (if you run a social media marketing agency) to edit and approve for scheduling. And the biggest thing that I wanted was to ensure that anyone could use it within minutes of opening it.

Steve Jobs said "Simple can be harder than complex: You have to work hard to get your thinking clean to make it simple. But it's worth it in the end because once you get there, you can move mountains."

This quote was my guiding compass in every decision we made for Social Labyrinth and everything we do at VENTUREWRITE. Make it simple. Make it clean. Get it right.

Twitter Tools

Twitter has its own set of tools that can be very helpful. It doesn't allow you to schedule posts on the platform, but you can use every scheduler to do that and I recommend that you do so. You can tweet as many times as you want within a day, but the main thing is that you NEED to tweet often and in line with the trends of the day. So schedule out a few tweets and then tweet in the moment when you have a free moment.

Tweetdeck is another tool that I use for Twitter. It is very similar to Hootsuite, but if you only need one tool to monitor your Twitter feed then this one is excellent. It is only available on your desktop so that is one drawback if you use multiple devices. The other tool I use for Twitter has nothing to do with scheduling tweets but allowing others to tweet from a blog – Click to Tweet. This is a great little tool that allows you to highlight a certain section of your blog and then make it easy for those reading it to share that small section with their Twitter followers. It doesn't take long to set up and can easily make your blogs more interactive and get more exposure.

One of the most important things you can do on Twitter besides following others, is to un-follow accounts. Twitter is full of inactive accounts and if you don't police your follows in the beginning you could end up following inactive accounts or spam accounts. I personally use Crowdfire and an app on my iPad called Unfollow. Both are free accounts for minimal use or can be upgraded to a paid version if you need to unfollow more accounts at a time or want additional services from the app.

There are more tools available out there such as ones that will collect stories and create newsletters from your followers' tweets or ones that create Twitter communities. Finding the tool that is right for your use is something that you need to discover through trial and error. Looking to do something specific on Twitter? Google it. I'm sure there is a tool for that.

Instagram and Schedulers

Instagram is one platform that does not like to be scheduled. It is something that they have railed against because they want the posting to be organic. They want a business or individual to be online, in the moment, responding and reacting to the latest content. This makes sense. Yet it makes it a bit more difficult to post consistently if it isn't top of mind.

The only scheduler that sort of allows you to post to Instagram is Hootsuite and even that doesn't really work. It allows you to set up the post but then it sends you an alert saying you can post it now. I just set an alarm on my phone and it works just as well.

Will Instagram work with schedulers someday? Maybe. But right now, it's a live, in the moment app. So follow its lead and LIVE IN THE MOMENT.

I will however, give you a tip. There are going to be similar accounts to yours that will post at a certain time. Their accounts will possibly be older than yours if you are just joining the platform and they will have tested their posting times already. You can set a notification to let you know when someone you are following has posted. When they post, you get a notification and then YOU POST AT THE SAME TIME. Scheduling and posting worries solved. You will also be piggy backing on the target audience that the account you followed is posting to, so be sure to use at least one of the same hashtags to get to them.

Curation Tools

There are some tools out there that just make your life easier. I like those tools.

Curation tools fall into this category. These are apps or websites that will gather information for you into a type of easy to read magazine based on a specific subject. Depending on the tool, they will use published articles from magazines and news outlets, with blogs and other high readership sites, or they may just pull from blogs.

My two favorites are Flipboard and Feedly.

Flipboard allows you to pull from anywhere on the web and add your own articles to what they call magazines. These are usually published in magazines, news articles or other large readership mediums. You can add stories to your magazines from others that have posted in their magazines, add articles you find and share your magazines with others to create a shared one.

This is an excellent tool to use when you want to pull a ton of articles together in one space for you to post to your social media account. The idea is to find something other than the mainstream articles that have the power to be shared. You can post articles from any website into your Flipboard magazines, so if you have a blog then you should also share it here.

Feedly is designed for blogs. You can search on a specific type of blog and it will come up from their RSS feeds and tell you how many readers a blog may have. You could argue that the more popular the blog the better it is, but I don't always follow that thought process. Some smaller blogs are only beginning, and others aren't interested in promotion. Therefore, they may have a smaller follower count yet provide excellent content.

Check out anything in your subject matter and subscribe to the blogs. The current articles will be pulled into your "feed" and you can browse and determine if there is anything worth sharing.

There are new curation tools that pop up daily. When I purchased my new iPhone I started to use the News app. It's just like every other curation tool. Choose categories and it will find mainly news stories and magazine articles, but information from influential blogs as well. It is quickly becoming one of my favorite morning rituals – coffee and the news app.

Other options are apps such as Nuzzel – which notifies you of the top tweeted stories from your network and puts it in a digest. This basically lets you know if you need to hop online and join in the conversation about something that may be going viral in your industry.

Right Relevance is one that attempts to find influencers in your specific industry and offer popular articles from them that they are sharing. This is one that I have used the least, but from time to time has some decent information and effectively stays on the subjects I have outlined.

Any tool that can make your life easier is fantastic in my book. Yet remember, while content curation is a necessary aspect to any online social media presence, it will always take the back seat to posting anything organic.

#SocialFAIL: Nothing Organic in your feed

I have had an account or two that will leave the posting entirely up to myself and my team. While this sounds like an excellent idea, there is one major flaw with this plan. They usually don't send us anything organic either. Posting organic - something that has come from your office, warehouse, in the field, etc, pictures of you and your team, is a baseline need for all social media platforms. People want to get to know the people behind the brand. You are more than a logo – show it!

The accounts with nothing organic? Even with ads, they have stayed stagnant for months and we eventually had to terminate the contracts. We love to help a business drive results on social – without some type of organic posting, we know that it is a uphill climb where the top is rarely, if ever, reached.

Excellence is about fighting and pursuing something diligently with a strict and determined approach to doing it RIGHT.
- Charlie Trotter

Social Media is So Much More than a Like

"A brand is no longer what we tell the consumer it is –
it is what consumers tell each other it is."
– Scott Cook

Social Media is more than a like or a follow.

It is building reputations and creating relationships with others that may share your passions or need something that you represent. It is a space where you can go to seek out thousands, if not millions of people who share your values, your thoughts, those that will agree with you and others that will challenge the way you do things.

187

#SocialFAIL: Not being Authentic

People and companies are not perfect. We like to think we are and often that is all that we will show others on our social media profiles. One of my most epic fails was trying to show others only the good times. My child was perfect, I worked out every single day, I have never made a misstep on social media. Not true – not even close. Sharing your mistakes and your failures allows others to connect with you and show that you are REAL. As a company you can do the same. People want to know who is answering the phone. They want to see pictures of the people who are packing their products and delivering them with care. Remember, it's the people behind the brand that people want to see and hear their stories.

People have written thousands of articles on the dangers of social media, there have also been thousands of articles about the positive benefits of this new age of connectedness. Rarely is anyone more than an arms-length away from his or her phone – seriously, where is your phone right now?

This level of digital connection is excellent for businesses when they take the time to capitalize and connect with their target audience. Not knowing your audience, just posting without a strategy, randomly shooting out things from the hip and never thinking to go out and interact with your customers is how a social media presence for a company has failed, time and time again.

The negative reviews will pop up unnoticed. The comments about horrible customer service will fall on an inactive Facebook page or Twitter feed and others will see it. You may not, but your prospective clients might.

Truly managing a business' digital presence takes time and it's important to invest that time, every day, to build a stronger business in today's world. When it really matters – it's not about you, it's about building avenues for your clients to get to you and ensuring that when they do, they are taken care of. It's about listening and sharing, building relationships that will gain you the 20% of customers that drive the 80% of your sales.

Those few customers, the loyal, raving fans that you consistently engage with, are those that will drive your business. You don't have to have the most likes or followers, but you do need to have an extremely active page.

One client will consistently tell his customers, "if you have a question and we aren't open, shoot us a note on Facebook. We are here to help if you ever need it". When people are brewing beer, having a resource available outside of business hours is HUGE.

Do you have to be available 24/7 for your clients? No, but it is ideal to have someone make it look like you are.

Do you have the manpower to monitor your accounts day and night? Are you paying attention to the people who are commenting or liking your posts more than others? Do you send out a note just to say thank you or send them a free gift for being a loyal customer? How are you building those relationships?

These are the questions that accompany me every day and every night. How do you share your passions online in this fast paced digital world and ensure that people connect with you - because you are much more than a logo.

Social Media platforms are tools that are only as good as those using them. There is nothing inherently good or bad about Facebook. It is just a place online where people go to share information. How people use the platform – that is what defines its value.

You can double and even triple your business by using social media correctly in conjunction with other traditional marketing methods. But you need to invest, understand and believe in the process. You need to be consistent and be there for the long haul.

Can you run social media for your own company? Absolutely. The question remains...should you? Only you can decide.

Enjoy the online world. Connect, drive your business and embrace the power of being social.

Are you looking for someone to coach your team on how to conquer your social media space or a knowledgeable company to create a consistent and strong presence for you? I am always looking for new connections! You can find me on the below social platforms:

*Facebook: www.facebook.com/VENTUREWRITEMEDIA

Instagram: @venturewritemedia

LinkedIn: www.linkedin.com/AngelaDenton

*Website: www.venturewrite.com

*Facebook messenger or the contact form on my website are the two best ways to reach me.

Good Luck in your business and may it thrive on social!

AKNOWLEDGEMENTS

I had a great deal of help in making this book a reality.

The amazing support and guidance of my coach, Matt Kinsella, is truly the reason that this is finally in print. It was a textbook case of social media networking – we connected on Twitter, became friends on Facebook, I read his book and a new business partnership was formed. He has led me to many insights and helped my business grow in ways I would have never have thought of when I started this journey. Thank you.

To my editors who each have their own issues with words and phrases – thank you for willing to read about something that you had absolutely no interest in. Dana, Roberta and Dave – I greatly appreciate all of your efforts.

To my clients who were the greatest inspiration for this book, I am eternally grateful for your business and the challenges that you provide. Every day is unique and exciting as we figure out a new path on this ever-changing roller coaster of social media marketing. Thank you for being a part of the VENTUREWRITE family.

And to the one man who constantly kept asking me — "why aren't you writing"? I finally made it happen Daddy, thank you for always believing in me.

Made in the USA
San Bernardino, CA
20 February 2020